Look Up, Loo

by Annette Smith
Photography by John Pettitt

NELSON PRICE MILBURN

Teddy bear hunt,
teddy bear hunt,
we are going
on a teddy bear hunt.

This is **my** clue.

<u>Clue</u>

Can you find a teddy bear?
Go out to the garden.
Look up on the swing.

This is **my** clue.

<u>Clue</u>

Can you find a teddy bear?
Go into the house.
Look down in the basket.

This is **my** clue.

Clue

Can you find a teddy bear?
Go out to the garden.
Look up on the chair.

This is **my** clue.

<u>Clue</u>

Can you find a teddy bear?
Go into the house.
Look down in the toy box.

Here is
my teddy bear.

My teddy bear
is up
on the swing.

I can see
my teddy bear.

My teddy bear
is down
in the basket.

My teddy bear is here.

My teddy bear is up on the chair.

Look at
my teddy bear.

My teddy bear
is down
in the toy box.

Teddy bear hunt,
teddy bear hunt,
we all went
on a teddy bear hunt.